Butterfly Colors

by Helen Frost

Consulting Editor: Gail Saunders-Smith, Ph.D.

Consultant: Dr. Ronald L. Rutowski,
Professor of Biology, Arizona State University

Pebble Books

an imprint of Capstone Press
Mankato, Minnesota

Pebble Books are published by Capstone Press
151 Good Counsel Drive, P.O. Box 669, Mankato, Minnesota 56002
http://www.capstone-press.com

3 4 5 6 04 03 02

Library of Congress Cataloging-in-Publication Data
Frost, Helen, 1949–
    Butterfly colors/by Helen Frost.
    p. cm.—(Butterflies)
    Includes bibliographical references and index.
    Summary: Examines the colors and patterns of various butterfly wings.
    ISBN 0-7368-0226-6
    1. Butterflies—Anatomy—Juvenile literature. 2. Wings—Juvenile literature.
[1. Butterflies.] I. Title. II. Series: Frost, Helen, 1949– Butterflies.
QL544.2.F76 1999
595.78'9—dc21   98-31720
                                               CIP
                                             AC

Note to Parents and Teachers

The Butterflies series supports national science standards related to the diversity and unity of life. This book describes the patterns and colors that appear on butterfly wings. The photographs support early readers in understanding the text. The repetition of words and phrases helps early readers learn new words. This book also introduces early readers to subject-specific vocabulary words, which are defined in the Words to Know section. Early readers may need assistance to read some words and to use the Table of Contents, Words to Know, Read More, Internet Sites, and Index/Word List sections of the book.

Table of Contents

4

Butterfly wings have many scales.

6

Each scale is one color.

8

The scales make butterfly
wings colorful.

blue pansy butterfly

10

Butterfly wings can be one color.

Julia butterfly

Butterfly wings can have patterns.

lacewing butterfly

The patterns can be spots.

tailed jay butterfly

The patterns can
be stripes.

zebra butterfly

A butterfly has two wings
on each side of its body.

great spangled fritillary butterfly

20

The two sides match.

golden banded forester butterfly

Words to Know

butterfly—a thin insect with large, colored wings; between 15,000 and 20,000 kinds of butterflies live in the world.

match—to be the same; the wings on one side of a butterfly's body are the same colors and pattern as the wings on the other side.

pattern—a repeated arrangement of colors and shapes; patterns help butterflies communicate with one another, warn enemies, or hide from enemies.

scales—small pieces of hard skin that cover a butterfly's wings; each scale is smaller than a grain of sand.

stripe—a narrow band of color; some butterflies have striped wings.

wing—the movable part of a butterfly that allows it to fly; butterfly wings are delicate and can tear in the wind.

Read More

Cassie, Brian. *The Butterfly Alphabet Book.* Watertown, Mass.: Charlesbridge, 1995.

Delafosse, Claude. *Butterflies.* A First Discovery Book. New York: Scholastic, 1996.

Saunders-Smith, Gail. *Butterflies.* Animals: Life Cycles. Mankato, Minn.: Pebble Books, 1997.

Stefoff, Rebecca. *Butterfly.* Living Things. New York: Benchmark Books, 1997.

Internet Sites

All About Butterflies
http://www.enchantedlearning.com/subjects/butterfly

Butterfly Collection
http://www.smm.org/sln/tf/links/butterfly.html

The Butterfly Website
http://butterflywebsite.com

Index/Word List

Word Count: 52
Early-Intervention Level: 11

Editorial Credits
Colleen Sexton, editor; Steve Christensen, cover designer; Kimberly Danger and Sheri Gosewisch, photo researchers

Photo Credits
David F. Clobes, 18
GeoImagery/Fi Rust, 8, 12, 14, 20
James P. Rowan, 16
Kate Boykin, cover
Photobank/Kjell Sandved, 6
Photri-Microstock, Inc./Rob Simpson, 10
Robert McCaw, 1
Unicorn Stock Photos/Ron Holt, 4